OUR
WORDS
MATTER

PALMETTO
P U B L I S H I N G
Charleston, SC
www.PalmettoPublishing.com

Copyright © 2024 by Dr. Dee Stern

All rights reserved

No portion of this book may be reproduced, stored in a retrieval system, or transmitted in any form by any means–electronic, mechanical, photocopy, recording, or other–except for brief quotations in printed reviews, without prior permission of the author.

Paperback ISBN: 979-8-8229-5572-1

OUR WORDS MATTER

CONSEQUENCES OF OUR WORDS

DR. DEE STERN

ACKNOWLEDGMENTS

I would like to thank and express a great deal of gratitude to those friends and colleagues, as well as the Bereaved in my grief and suicide groups and a former student who encouraged me to write a third book, because it was a book that had to be written.

My Lord, thank you for your support, encouragement, and surprises along the way, as I wrote my third book. Without you, I would never have had the wisdom or strength to start, and finish this book.

Janet Zimmerman, a close friend and my tech support, who put up with my frustrations with the computer and who supported me when the computer took over and I was completely lost again. Without Janet's assistance and encouragement, I would never have been able to comprehend the workings of the computer and proceed and finish this project.

Linda Hughes, a good friend and computer wizard, who once again rescued me from problems and questions I had on the computer concerning my book.

Lesley Wolfgang, a friend and colleague, who encouraged me from day one to write this book, because it had to be written. Her listening ear, gentle advice, support and help with locating articles and giving me examples were of exceptional help and allowed me to make this book authentic and stay on track when I seemed to wonder off.

Carol Moore, a good friend, whose excitement for the book being written, her encouragement, her listening ear, her gentleness, helped me through her support and prayers by always encouraging me to continue to write this book because it had to be written.

Darlene Cockayne, a former student, encouraged me to keep going and not give up.

Jeff Koester, a good friend and a physical therapist whose friendship, prayers, enthusiasm, and excitement about the book and his many encouraging words gave me the support and strength, I needed at times to continue writing and finishing this book.

To the many bereaved that hopefully one day, people will think before they speak to you and cause you less pain than you are already experiencing.

Blessings and Thanks and much Gratitude to all of you for your support and confidence in me as this book came together.

TABLE OF CONTENTS

INTRODUCTION 1

OUR WORDS MATTER 1

DO OUR WORDS MATTER? 7

WORDS AND ACTIONS 11

DO MEN GET THE SUPPORT THEY TRULY NEED WHEN A CHILD DIES? 17

WHAT HAPPENS WHEN WE DON'T TALK ABOUT OUR PAIN? 21

WHY DON'T WE SAY THE NAMES OF PEOPLE WHO HAVE DIED? 25

SHOULD WE HAVE FUNERALS? 29

WHAT YOU NEED TO KNOW AS YOU TRY TO NAVIGATE THROUGH
YOUR GRIEF JOURNEY 33

TO THE NEWLY BEREAVED 37

SHOULD CHILDREN BE TOLD WHEN A DEATH OCCURS? 43

WHO ARE THE FORGOTTEN SURVIVORS? 47

WHAT DO ADOLESCENTS WANT FROM US WHEN THEY ARE
EXPERIENCING A DIFFICULT TIME IN THEIR LIVES?................... 51

TIPS FOR PARENTS WHEN THERE HAS BEEN A DEATH................ 55

HAVE YOU EVER HAD A LOVED ONE WHO ENDED THEIR LIFE?........... 61

TALKING TO ADOLESCENTS ABOUT SUICIDE 67

DO YOU THINK YOU MIGHT NEED TO TALK WITH SOMEONE SINCE
YOUR LOVED ONE DIED?... 71

WHY DO WE NEED SUPPORT WHEN WE ARE GRIEVING? 75

WHAT IS A GRIEF SUPPORT GROUP? 79

DO YOU LISTEN TO WHAT YOUR DOG IS TRYING TO TELL YOU?
DO YOU UNDERSTAND THEIR SIGNALS?........................... 83

WHAT SHOULD YOU SAY TO SOMEONE WHOSE PET HAS DIED?........... 87

PETS GRIEVE TOO! 91

THE HOLIDAYS AND SOME IDEAS ON HOW TO GET THROUGH THEM 95

THE HOILDAYS AND WHY THEY CAN BE DIFFICULT.................... 99

TRIGGERS—ANNIVERSARIES, BIRTHDAYS, HOLIDAYS................. 105

DOES GRIEF STOP IN THE SUMMER TIME?.......................... 111

INTRODUCTION
OUR WORDS MATTER

What are the consequences of our words?

No matter what you say or who you say it to, your words can have consequences-good as well as bad. Words can make a difference in the person receiving your words, whether the words are loving or hateful –there will be a consequence and could change someone's life forever. Sometimes we may just not realize what affect we may be having on the other person receiving the message.

When I was growing up, I was told to think before I speak. Sounds easy, but it is not always easy to do.

Using the right language around children, no matter what their age, is also very important. Young children often take words literally. When a death occurs and they are told that, they must be the man of the house now that their dad has died and also to take care of their mom and their brothers and sisters. No matter their age, they feel they need to take over the chores, help make decisions and be sure mom is okay.

They may be told not to cry in front of their mom, because it could upset her----so out of fear of upsetting their mom and the family, they usually do not cry. This is a very big responsibility for a young child to take on, yet, these are the words said to them by a family member.

Now what does the child do with their grief? Who can they go to for help? Who can the child cry with or talk with about this loss?

When a child or teen goes on line and says things to bully another child or teen –the person who reads it will be different forever and what they read could even eventually end in a suicide.

When you tell a bereaved person to "Move on," or to "Get over it," you could be causing them more pain than before you said anything to them. Often the bereaved may feel that you don't care, otherwise, you wouldn't be rushing them through their grief. Are you telling them to "move on" and "get over it," because you are uncomfortable seeing their sadness, or are you really concerned about this bereaved person?

Other examples of our words hurting the bereaved are: "Now that your spouse died, you will have more time for your friends," "You are young enough, you can find someone else," "Sorry to hear that your brother died, but you do have a large family and other siblings who care about you." "I am going to pray for you, because your son has been dammed to Hell," (that comment came after he ended his life.) "Aren't you glad your baby died you don't know what it would have grown up to be like?" All of these words are real comments that were said to the bereaved.

How sad the bereaved were left with those words while the persons who said them went on their way, perhaps not realizing the pain they had left behind or the consequences of those words.

It is very important to realize that Our words can bring joy or pain to someone.

So, what is the point that I am trying to make? It is that no matter who you are or who you speak to, it is important to think before you speak, because words like Love, Hate, Death, Sex, bullying someone, can change you and the person or persons' who hear these words forever.

So, how can your language, your words, be comforting to someone who is grieving? What would you want someone to say to you after a death of your loved one? What would bring you comfort?

Often just being a good listener without offering any advice can be better than any words you could ever say to them.

Allow the bereaved to feel what they feel without telling them how they should feel or that they should stop thinking or talking about their loved one, because it only makes them sad.

You can make a difference in the lives of your colleagues, family, friends and especially to the bereaved, if you simply take a moment or two to care about the words you are about to say to someone who has just had a death.

If you understand what I am trying to say, perhaps you too can become an active advocate for listening and thinking before you speak. Just think of the many lives you could change for the better.

For you see, when one person changes there is a chance that motion will ricochet to others who will continue to pass that on to others who will begin to see a difference and then they too will think before they speak.

What a beautiful world we could begin to live in. To talk to each other, listen to each other and help each other. I know you might be thinking this is silly and it won't happen, but it can. Thanks for at least giving it a chance to work.

In the midst of a lot of negative words, I try to look for a glimmer of hope which is the message of this book that will reach enough people to make a difference.

This book is not a mystery thriller, a romance novel, or a book on sex, but rather one that can make a difference in everyone's life and the people they speak to everyday and hopefully in the future as well.

The problem with negative words, is that people tend to remember them rather than positive words, and carry these negative words with them where ever they go. These negative words can cause unhappiness, mental as well as physical problems that can turn into even bigger problems along the way.

It is very important for the bereaved or those hurting to say what they want or need from others so that the messages are delivered with comforting words rather than hurtful words. Sometimes just a shoulder to cry on is needed, sometimes a listening ear (without advice) and maybe even just a hug is all that is needed.

Perhaps a phone call now and then to ask what the bereaved might need or would they like to go out for a meal sometime. Telling them you are praying for them (but be sure you are, because they are depending on your prayers to help them get through some of their difficult times), is a wonderful thing to say to them.

Blessings to all of you as you take time to listen to the bereaved.

NOTE: As you read these essays you may notice I have used several words over and over such as "Move ON" and "Get Over it." This was done on purpose to get a point across that these are words that many people use when talking to the bereaved, which can cause more pain than comfort to them and should not be used.

Other words that you may be seeing several times is: How grief affects people when they are grieving, is also very important, such as: physically, mentally, socially and spiritually.

And to "THINK BEFORE YOU SPEAK," because "OUR WORDS DO MATTER."

DO OUR WORDS MATTER?

What do our words mean when we are talking to someone? Our words often cause an action or a reaction from the receiver. Our words can be loving, sweet, caring or possibly harsh, vindictive, cruel, or uncaring.

I believe most people really don't realize the effect their words have on another person, they simply say what they want and move on, not realizing the impact of what was just said. As a grief therapist, for many years, I have found this to be very true when someone is speaking to the bereaved.

It seems that when some people talk with the bereaved, they are trying to help them, but in reality, they are causing them more hurt than true concern. It also seems that sometimes the non-bereaved person is giving the bereaved advice as to how to feel, how to act, and what to do with their life, after a death such as "Get Over IT", or "Move on." However, in reality they are feeling uncomfortable with the way the bereaved are crying a lot, their sadness, and loneliness and want them to change to make the non-bereaved to feel better.

Many times, the non-bereaved person will give their advice and then go home to their spouse, friend, child, or sibling who is living and feels good about their advice to the bereaved whose, loved one has died and the bereaved individual is now left to deal with the words just left behind.

Grief is a very difficult process to try to navigate through, so when someone does not understand or feels uncomfortable—words can often leave the bereaved worse than they were before.

So, what can be done to help those who are non-bereaved to try to understand that their words could hurt rather than help someone who has just experienced a death in their life? There are seven easy things that help the non-bereaved and the bereaved at the same time. They are:

First and foremost; THINK BEFORE YOU SPEAK!

Second: LISTEN RATHER THAN SPEAK!

Third: What would you want someone to say to you if you had experienced the death of a loved one?

Fourth: Remember, this could be You someday.

Fifth: Sometimes Silence or a Hug may be better than words can convey. However, be sure to ask the person if you could give them a hug, because they may not want you to.

Sixth: If you offer to pray for them and their family, please be sure that you do, because they will be expecting you to pray for them.

Seventh: Always try to mention the deceased person's name when talking to the bereaved. If possible, tell the bereaved a story or something that you remember about the deceased.

All of these items help the bereaved to feel that their loved one has not been forgotten and that someone still remembers them, and that they have been heard.

The words we say to the bereaved or anyone else really, can cause a great deal of joy, or a great deal of sadness. Remember the 7 items just mentioned before you speak words that can possibly be words that you cannot take back or that will not be forgotten and will live on in a person's mind every time, they see you or think about you.

Words like: "I love you," "I care about you," "I am here for you," "I will pray for you" are always appreciated.

Words such as: "Why can't you just listen, instead of always trying to fix things?" "What really happened?" "Move on!" "Get over it!" "You have children who need you." "You are young enough you can always find someone else." When a pet dies, "You can always go out and get another one -it was only an animal."

"Time heals all wounds" or "It was God's Will!"

Why do some people say and act the way they do sometimes? Some don't think, some don't care, some really care but are not really sure what to say, so they often say the wrong thing.

Words matter and can be very powerful. People are hurt everyday by someone who is upset, hurt, or just doesn't care about what they say and certainly do not realize the consequences of their words.

To close, Please, remember that YOUR WORDS MATTER and the Seven items mentioned earlier will help you as you help the bereaved to navigate through their journey of grief in a smoother and healthier way. Thank you!

Blessings to all of you!!!

WORDS AND ACTIONS

I have talked about our words and the difference they can make when talking with the bereaved. I would like to go even further.

What do you say or not say when someone is hurting inside and afraid or unsure about asking for help? Would you listen or would you say what you think they should hear? What action would you take? Sometimes our actions speak louder than words.

To "spill your guts" to someone takes a lot of trust and faith in that person that they will "not think less of you," "ignore you," or "give you advice -that you did not ask for," but rather just listen.

Just having someone who cares enough about you to listen and not judge you, can make a big difference in your recovery and your trust level. Many times, words can get in the way, when having a hug, a shoulder to cry on, no advice (unless asked for) and someone to care about you by just listening to you at this very fragile time, means more than anything anyone could say.

What if someone is ill and asks to speak to the clergy, but the clergy is too busy or on a short schedule and feels they don't have the time to talk to anyone. Fortunately, most clergy would take the time to talk to someone, but there are also some that would not.

Our words and our actions matter and can help or hurt the person asking for help. If our words or actions communicate to the bereaved, that we are too busy to listen or to take some unplanned time to help them we could be making matters worse and could make them feel that they don't matter.

If someone cares about you, and wants to be around you in the "good times" as well as the "difficult times" and is willing to listen and be there for you, perhaps, this is the person to trust with your inner turmoil and pain and know you will be listened to and not judged or ignored.

If you were to go to a therapist—you must pay them to listen to you, but if there is no connection between the two of you-----you are wasting your money, and your time and their time. So going to the right therapist is also very important to get the help you may need.

So, what can you do and who can you trust, with your inner sadness?

First PRAY, then trust your "gut" to know who you should talk with. You know who has helped you in the past and listened to you and who has not. You know who is a casual friend and who is someone you can trust, someone that will not judge, ignore or expect you to work this out on your own.

Remember a good rule is to think before you speak and listen as often as you can. Also, if it were you in this situation, what would you want someone to say to you or not to say to you? You really never know when you will be called upon to help------what will your action be? What will your words be?

Words can bring comfort or pain and suffering. The way we communicate with someone---the language we use----the words we choose are very important and can comfort someone or cause them pain and suffering. Sometimes we may just say something and not realize what affect we may be having on the other person receiving the message.

When I was growing up, I was always told to think before you speak. Sounds easy, but it is not always easy to do. It seems to be easier for introverts to do rather than extroverts, because many extroverts usually speak before they think about what they are going to say. However, it is not always easy for some introverts either.

Unfortunately, the bereaved are usually the ones who received unsolicitous advice as well as a lot of comments such as "You are young enough to find someone else." "Aren't you glad your baby died you don't know what it would have been like when it grew up." These words and others like them are often received by the bereaved and are certainly not comforting, but rather very hurtful to hear.

Using the right language around children no matter what age, is also very important. Young children often take words very literally. They are told not to cry in front of their mom because it might upset her, so out of fear of upsetting mom and the family, they don't cry. This is a very big responsibility for a young child to take on, yet that might be the words told to them from a family member.

Now what does the child do with their grief? Who is there to help them? Who can they cry with or talk with about their loss?

Why do some people feel the need to just speak and have no idea how they could be hurting the one person they are trying to comfort? Today, more people are texting and not even talking face to face, yet sending words of comfort without realizing the consequences that there may be to their words.

So, how can language ---words be comforting to someone who is grieving?

One way is to think before you speak.

Think what would help you if you were grieving? What words would you like to hear from someone that would bring you comfort?

Often being a good listener without offering any advice is better than any words you could ever say to anyone who is hurting.

Allowing someone to feel what they feel without telling them how they should feel or that they should stop thinking or talking about their deceased loved one and move on.

So, trying to think before you speak and the words you are about to use, will make a big difference to whoever you try to comfort. You could make a big difference in the lives of your colleagues, family, friends and especially the bereaved, if you simply take a moment or two to care about the language you are about to speak.

Often people just don't know what to say to the bereaved, so they say what they think will make them feel better, which doesn't always turn out very comforting.

Have you ever thought about how a person might feel after you leave them and you have just given them unsolicitous advice and you have caused them a lot of hurt. I think most people do not think about that.

A bereaved person in my grief group told me, after a while, it is not what someone said to her that she will remember and might forget later, but rather how they made her feel after they gave her advice that she did not ask for.

She told me, the advice that was given to her at the visitation, was so hurtful, she will always remember how she felt, even after two years of her loved one's death. She went on to say, that every time she sees that person, it all comes back to her over and over again.

I think it is important to remember that when you offer someone advice or unsolicitous advice, that perhaps, it might make you feel good, but it does not always work that way for the person receiving your words.

Again. THINK BEFORE YOU SPEAK and BEAWARE OF YOUR WORDS!!!!!!!!!!!! Blessings to all of you who listen and take the time to think before you speak!!!!!

DO MEN GET THE SUPPORT THEY TRULY NEED WHEN A CHILD DIES?

The answer to that is not really. When a little boy falls they are told to "suck it up," "Don't be a crybaby, remember, you have to be tough." They are basically told by society to stuff their feelings because they have to be tough and not cry like a little girl might do. Now they don't know what to do with these feeling, except they are not allowed to express them in public.

Now this little boy has grown to be a teenager and his best friend has been killed in an automobile crash, died from drug over dose or perhaps someone in his family has died. He has no idea what to do with his feelings or who to talk to because he has never been allowed to express them.

This teenager is now a young man in his 20's and he has had other experiences of death and grief throughout his life and still not sure what to do. Then a sibling, close friend, or parent ends their life and he is devasted. He ends up going to a therapist for help, but the words and feelings are just not coming and he sits in silence for fear of what the therapist might think of him.

This young man is now in his 30's-40's and is married and has a family and one of his children dies from a disease, an accident or ended his life. His wife had a miscarriage and everyone is surrounding her trying to comfort her. BUT he is the dad and that was to be his child too. His wife and family are trying to comfort him but he is not sure what to say, except he is in a great deal of pain inside and no one will listen to him. He wants to scream, cry, shout but doesn't know what to do, because he has been told as a little boy to be "tough," "don't cry or show your feelings, that is not what a big boy does."

He just wants to be heard and express his pain and sorrow and grief for his own flesh and blood, but how does he do that and who will really listen to him. Sometimes he thinks that the answer is to just get drunk and that way, he won't feel the pain. Perhaps he should just work a lot and don't think about the death, but that doesn't work either.

He started to cry, but quickly wiped his eyes from his inner pain and the loss of his child. His wife and family were allowed to cry, mourn and grieve, so why wasn't he?

There are misconceptions by many people about grief, that after a few months we are to "Move on" and simply "Get over it." How sad that many people are treated this way, especially men. They need help, support and comfort just like everyone else and sometimes even more.

The man has always been thought of as being the strong one of the family and he should have a "stiff upper Lip." How sad that men are treated like that most of the time. How sad that they are forgotten when it comes to grief. They need to know and be told they are not alone and people are praying for them too, but most of all they need to be heard and allowed to express their feelings outwardly and not ignored or ridiculed if they show their emotions, but rather supported and comforted.

Remember, to allow men to feel what they feel and allow them to express their inner turmoil and grief as they try to navigate their way through their journey of grief. Hopefully, as we do this to support them, they too will reach out to other men as well as their own siblings, children and grandchildren to support and show their love to them as well.

WHAT HAPPENS WHEN WE DON'T TALK ABOUT OUR PAIN?

I have written before about how our words matter, but what if you Don't express your words—your pain, your feelings of loss, anger, emptiness, sadness? What, could happen to you if you don't deal with the pain of your deceased loved one?

Why is it so important to speak about your deceased loved one to family and others.? Could this result in problems mentally, physically, socially, or even spiritually?

The answer is Yes, it could affect you in many different ways. The problem is that many times there are families that want to protect their family from the pain of death, so no one is allowed to talk about their loved one who died for fear of causing more pain to the family. This in itself could cause more problems in the future, especially if children or teens are involved.

They can become confused with how they feel and who they can go to talk with about how they are feeling, and especially since they are not allowed to cry or speak of the deceased.

As they grow up, they take all this pain with them and do not talk about their pain or feelings when someone else close to them dies. Can they go to their teacher or a counselor and tell them how sad they are because their loved one or a friend has died? Yes, but, maybe out of fear that their teacher or counselor will contact their family and they might get in trouble, they might feel uncomfortable talking with them.

Maybe they could talk to one of their close friends about what they are experiencing. This is possible, but what if that person tells their family because they are concerned about how their friend is feeling and the family contacts that family to offer their concern and the teen or child could perhaps get in trouble for bothering another family with their problems.

As you can see this can go on and on and get very complicated and can certainly cause-mentally, physically, socially and even spiritual problems down the road.

Now the child/ teen is an adult. I have had several of these adults in my grief and suicide (for family and friends who have already ended their lives) groups in these situations where the adult is now married with children of their own and are trying to figure out how to help their children with the loss of a loved one and don't know what to say to them, because they were never allowed to express their grief many years ago.

These adults didn't know how to express their sadness, pain, love and guilt, because they were never allowed to and now, that they are parents, they are confused as to what and how to talk to their children about death and the grief that often goes with it.

I had a young man in my suicide group at the end of one of our sessions, who said, this was the first time anyone had ever listened to his fears and sadness that he had been carrying around with him for many years.

Even friends and family tell the bereaved to "move on," and "get over it."

It is very important and OKAY to talk about your fears, your sadness, your guilt feelings, your anger, and the pain you might be feeling due to the loss of a family member, a friend or even a family pet. It is important to tell your story over and over again. It is okay to cry or not cry. It is OKAY NOT TO BE OKAY!!!!!

It is NOT OKAY to keep all these feelings inside, because they can cause physical, mental and social problems and even spiritual problems now and in the future.

So, please, allow yourself to feel what you feel and share those feelings with someone who will listen to you and perhaps give you the help you may need, then you too will be able to help yourself as well as your children when a death occurs.

WHY DON'T WE SAY THE NAMES OF PEOPLE WHO HAVE DIED?

Several people have written poems about saying the name of a person or telling a story about a loved one after they died. These poems are vital to most of the bereaved, because they explain what it means to the bereaved to hear their loved one's name mentioned and to know that they are not forgotten.

It seems like there is a myth that if someone should mention the name or a memory of the bereaved deceased loved one's they will be hurt, sad, or even devastated to hear this. However, the truth is just the opposite.

So, why don't we say the deceased names or talk about them after a death? Is it that we are afraid it will hurt or upset their loved ones who are left? Is it that we are too busy with our own lives, that we have moved on? Is it that we just don't care? Is it that we just don't feel comfortable talking about someone who has died?

After our loved one dies, it is so important to know that they will not be forgotten by others. When we hear others talk about them, hear their name mentioned or hear stories about them it feels good and gives us hope to know they will not be forgotten and perhaps that they even made a difference.

I believe we live in a death-denying society where people are afraid to talk about someone who died or reach out to friends or family members of those who have died. All of this is so sad because the bereaved are the ones who are truly suffering from the loss of their loved one and many times the support they need and want is just not given. A simple word or a kind gesture can go a long way to reassure the bereaved they are not alone in their grief.

As a grief therapist, LCPC, psychologist and chaplain in a hospital where I facilitate three grief groups---one weekly grief support group, an SOS (survivors of suicide—for family and friends of those who have already died by suicide) every first and third week of the month, a weekly children/teen grief support group and also some private counseling as well; over the years, I have seen and heard the tears, anger and pain of the bereaved whether it be from a Covid-19 death, cancer, heart attack, suicide etc. They are lost, lonely and longing to hear someone talk about their loved one in a conversation, or hear a story or memory about them that they had not heard before or even a familiar memory of their loved one.

The pain they feel is very deep and their sadness, anxiety and anger they experience is at times overwhelming. The bereaved simply cannot understand why their friends, family or even colleagues and physicians don't mention their deceased loved ones when they talk with them.

How to Help the Bereaved

So, what can we do to reach out to the bereaved? First, it is extremely important for the bereaved to talk about their loved ones around other people which in turn will give others permission to talk about them with the bereaved.

Next, everyone else simply needs to talk about the bereaved loved one's in a conversation or share a story or memory of what you remember about them. By doing this you are bringing them joy that their loved one has not been forgotten and that others really do care about them. If the bereaved do break down and cry, they are tears of happiness that their loved one is being remembered. Also please be patient with them and think, how that would make you feel if your loved one died and no one remembered your loved one?

It is sad to think that sometimes, a family member or friend has to die before someone actually understands what the bereaved go through. As my grief groups would say, they just don't get it! Remember, it is in the telling of your story that your healing takes place.

SHOULD WE HAVE FUNERALS?

The question in this Blog, "Should we have funerals?" may seem like a strange question, but today in this complicated world that we live in – is it really a strange question? I don't think so. So then why do we still have funerals? Are funerals for the living or the dead? What do you think?

According to Dr. William G. Hoy, there are four reasons: to "Remember, Reaffirm, Realize and Release."

The first reason is to Remember: Remember means exactly what it says. We remember through pictures, stories, music, eulogies from the clergy (if there is one present) or from perhaps a family member or friend who knew the deceased. We relive stories of our deceased loved one at the visitation, the funeral mass or church service as well as at the celebrations that follow the burial, such as the luncheons provided by the family or church.

Where else can you get a captive audience to reminisce about your deceased loved one? For some of those listening, it is really a time to remember, a time to laugh but also a time to cry. A time to think back about the stories they remember about the deceased. A time when perhaps, later they too can share their stories with the family and friends of the deceased.

It is a time to remember perhaps their loves, such as gardening, singing, sewing, photography, writing, sports, doing crafts or just being who they were with their children, grandchildren and perhaps even their great grandchildren.

The second is to Reaffirm: This means to perhaps find your way back to the spirituality that seems to have gone astray for a while, but now seems to be a necessity to help you get through this difficult time in your life. It might mean, to have a talk with the clergy, or a friend who you can talk to about how you are feeling and perhaps pray together for yourself and the deceased.

Perhaps It means joining a grief support group and finding out, that you are not the only one who feels the way you do as well as getting the help you need to get through this very difficult time.

The next is to Realize: To realize that we live in a death denying society where people don't talk about death or the dying and therefore, they make it very difficult for someone to actually deal with the death of their loved one.

Today many children who don't go to church or Temple, feel their parent doesn't need a funeral service or Mass because they the children don't believe anymore, but yet their parent went to their church or Temple every week. How sad to deny their parent what they believed and practiced religiously, because it makes their children feel uncomfortable to walk into a church or Temple even for a funeral.

The last one is to Release: Is to say goodbye to our loved one. Saying good bye does not however, mean we will forget our deceased loved one or that our grief is over after the funeral or burial. It means it is really the continuation of our grief, which began when our loved one died or in some cases before their death occurred such as in ALS or Dementia.

Grief takes as long as it takes. We all grieve differently, what works for one person, doesn't necessarily work for someone else. Grief can take months to years to a lifetime, depending on the type of death and the age of the deceased.

Grief can cause the bereaved to have a difficult time trying to focus, to remember where we may have put things, to forget where we are going, etc. We may have headaches, heart problems, aches and pains we didn't have before, our immune system seems to be off somewhat.

We are not motivated to do anything, when before we were always on the go. We are tired all the time, don't feel like eating or can't stop eating. We might have trouble sleeping or sleeping too long and not wanting to get out of bed.

We may not want to be around others or call anyone to talk with. We may feel lonely as well as alone.

We may stop going to church or the Temple. We may blame God for our loved one's death. We may stop praying, because we have just plain given up on life- we have become depressed.

As we say our final goodbyes to our loved one our new normal has already begun to take over and perhaps, we may need to seek help in a month or so.

So, are funerals essential? Yes, for many reasons but it is also a time for Healing, Remembering, Reaffirming, Realizing and Releasing. Please allow yourself to feel what you feel and take your time to heal and to plan a funeral gathering.

WHAT YOU NEED TO KNOW AS YOU TRY TO NAVIGATE THROUGH YOUR GRIEF JOURNEY

Trying to navigate through your grief is not any easy thing to do—but I am sure you might know that by now.

I have many people who when they first come into my grief groups ask, "How long is this going to take—weeks, months, years?" My answer is always the same. "Grief takes as long as it takes." Now that may sound like I am trying to avoid the question-but I am not. Grief does take as long as it takes.

Everyone grieves differently, for example: men and women grieve differently, children and teens, older adults than younger adults do. There is no set time limit. What works for one person may not work for anyone else.

You see, when you have lost a piece of your heart, there is no time limit. There is no right way to grieve, just yours. If it works for you, that is great, however, if it doesn't perhaps you might try something different.

It might help you to do some journaling, to seek out a grief group or an individual grief therapist- remember, not every therapist works with grief, so be sure you find a grief therapist.

You might even look back into your life when you had another loss or something tragic and how you made it through that experience. What did you do then that you are not doing now?

It is important to also know, that it is okay NOT to be okay right now. There will be friends, neighbors, family members that may try to rush you through your grief—because they are uncomfortable with how you are acting, how you are feeling. PLEASE IGNORE THEM. THEY ARE NOT GRIEVING YOU ARE!!!!!

The way you grieve also depends on the type of death, whether it is medical, suicide, death of a baby, child, teen, pet, accident, grandparent, etc. It also depends on how close you were to the person who died. How old they were.

Was this a sudden death, a lingering illness, a shooting/stabbing. Were you with them when they died? Did they live out of town and you got a phone call about their death?

You will enter a "new normal" which means you cannot go back to the way things were in the past because your loved one has died and no longer here. However, you can still communicate with them.

In this "new normal" whatever you are feeling is okay. If you are crying a lot, feeling guilty, angry, not wanting to be around people, it is okay because that is where you are now and that is what grief is about.

Mentally, you may not be able to focus on what you are reading or doing at home or at your job. You may lose things, forget where you put things, go to the store and not remember why you went, drive down the street and not remember where you are going or how you even got there. THIS YOUR NEW NORMAL FOR AWHILE—but NOT FOREVER.

Grief can affect your life physically, mentally, socially, and spiritually. Please seek help, if you think you might need it. Don't let others tell you when they think you should get help, only you know when you are ready.

Physically, you may feel very tired, chest pain, headaches, aches and pains all over your body as well as other physical symptoms.

Socially, sometimes it takes a village to help you navigate through your grief and that is okay. Just remember, it may seem like you are alone—but when you ready to talk to someone, need a shoulder to cry on, someone to listen to you without giving you unsolicitous advice, or someone to just give you a hug there will be someone there to help you.

There are people in your life that you trust or that you didn't expect to be there for you, but they will be there for you—YOU ARE NOT ALONE, even though many times it may seem like it.

You may take one step forward and two steps back, but that is to be expected when you are trying to navigate through the muddy waters of grief.

Spiritually, you may not feel comfortable with how you are feeling about God, because you have been praying for your loved one and they died anyway. When you are ready, it may be a good idea to make an appointment to talk with your clergy. This might help you in some way.

You may not want to go back to your place of worship, because you may be afraid of crying around others. Perhaps going to a different service, might also help you as well.

So, don't give up, don't let others put expectations on you and your grief (I am sure you may have already done that to yourself) take a deep breath and talk about your loved one and allow others to do the same and your loved one will never be forgotten. It can be a wonderful feeling to hear stories about your loved one that you never heard before.

It is okay to tell your story, because it is in the telling of your story that your healing will take place.

Blessing to you as you navigate through your grief journey.

TO THE NEWLY BEREAVED

I am sorry for your loss and hope that you will find peace and comfort on your journey of grief. I hope this article helps you in some way to get through your grief. So, what is grief? Grief is one of the most difficult things to try to endure in your lifetime, because your loved one is no longer physically here, but you are. Your task is to go on living and dealing with life as it is now for you, however, this is easier to say than to actually do.

The first year of your loss can be very difficult, because it is a year of firsts—birthdays, anniversaries, holidays all without your loved one.

Grief can affect you physically, mentally, socially and spiritually. After a death, you will begin a new normal, which simply means, everything from here on out, whatever you think, and feel is now normal. You cannot go back to the way you were, because your loved one has died and you are now left to deal with whatever life hands you, with perhaps some support, but it is not the same without your loved one to talk to.

There will be others who are not bereaved and who will not understand why you are acting the way you are (such as crying a lot, not able to focus, tired a lot) and expect you to "Get over it" or "Move on" after a few weeks or months. Please do not listen to them, because grief takes as long as it takes and everyone grieves differently.

Please do not panic and think you are grieving wrong. If what you are doing seems to be helping you, you are on the right track, if not you might want to talk to someone about how you are dealing with your loved one's death. Remember, there is only one way to grieve and that is your way, if it works.

Many times, people who try to rush the bereaved through their grief, usually feel uncomfortable with the person who has experienced a loss and don't know what to do to help them and so they try to rush the bereaved along, so they, not the bereaved will feel better.

As you move on in your grief, you may feel anger at God, the doctors, your family or even your deceased loved one (especially if you feel they did not take care of themselves). You may feel guilty, and experience, would haves, could haves, or should haves and perhaps think you should have done more for your loved one, when in reality, you did everything you could possibly have done.

Physically and mentally, you could feel aches and pains that you have never experienced before or possibly had problems but you did not deal with them because you didn't want to leave your loved one, so instead, you put off going to the doctor.

You may feel tired all the time, have trouble sleeping, no appetite or can't stop eating, can't seem to focus, feel numb, can't remember where you are going or why you are going there.

You might decide to go to the store and not remember what you went for, so you decide to make a list next time and then you lose the list, losing objects a lot (such as keys, cell phones), are all very common during grief.

Socially, your friends may not want to be around you, because of your crying or wanting to talk about your deceased loved one. So, it is very important that you tell them what you want from them. When someone dies, we seem to lose all control of what to do or say. It is important to take that control back and tell your family and friends what you want from them. Perhaps you might just want someone to listen to you and not give you advice.

If someone asks you to go out for lunch and you don't want to go, then tell them you don't want to go this time, but perhaps another time, don't go to make them happy and yourself miserable. Always be honest with them. If you are having a bad day, tell them you are having a bad day, and you just don't feel like talking right now, you don't have to explain anything to them unless you feel the need to.

It is important to be honest with your family/ children, and friends and allow them to see you cry, by doing this you are giving them permission to grieve with you as well and not try to hide their feelings every time they see you. If someone should ask you how you are doing, please DO NOT SAY I AM FINE OR OKAY, because you are not. When you tell someone that, they may feel you are doing good and that you are back to your old self, and then they will not be able to understand why this GRIEF THING is taking you so long to get through.

So be HONEST with everyone, both you and those not bereaved will benefit from your honesty.

Spiritually, you may blame God for your loved one dying, when you prayed all the time and they still died. You may not want to go back to church or the Temple for fear you may cry and people will stare at you. You may not want to return, because you are unable to find any meaning in your life right now and see no need to go back to church or the Temple.

Sometimes it helps to seek out the clergy and talk with them, sometimes it helps to go back to church or the Temple, but either go at another time or go to a different place to worship where no one knows you.

Grief is like a roller coaster. One day you may be feeling better and things seem to be looking up and the next day you spend crying. It may feel like you take one step forward and two steps back.

The main thing is Never Give Up!! Remember, Grief takes as long as it takes, so please don't put expectations on yourself, because there are plenty of people around you who already do that.

However, you could make an appointment to talk with a grief counselor, or join a grief group and tell your story—remember it is in the telling of the story that the healing takes place. The more you keep all your feelings inside, the longer it takes to get through your loss. There is an old saying that Time heals all things, this is not really true, rather it is what you do with that time.

It is a good idea to make an appointment to see your doctor after at least 6 weeks, just to check on how you are doing. It is possible they are not even aware your loved one died. Please be aware of how much medication they give you, and don't over medicate yourself. As you go through your grief, you should be able to know what you are doing and not be so drugged you are unable to function.

In conclusion: take one day at a time and go from there! On those days when it is too hard to put one foot in front of the other—take a deep breath, try to rest and relax, call someone you trust to listen to you, but mainly do something that gives you peace and comfort.

Remember you are not alone in this thing called GRIEF. Blessings to you as you walk, stumble and get up again and keep walking on your journey of grief. Remember, you don't get over a death—you get through it and you will!!

SHOULD CHILDREN BE TOLD WHEN A DEATH OCCURS?

The answer to that question is Yes. The other day I came across an article about a young married couple who disagree on how to tell or not tell their Children (when they have them) about death and grieving.

I began to think about how many other parents and grandparents disagree on what to tell their children and grandchildren about a death; as well as how many children and teens often do not receive the correct language about dying and death.

I understand that parents and grandparents want to protect their children and grandchildren from death and from being sad or hurt when a death occurs, however, when a death does occur, it is very important that the children /teens are made aware of who died and to be able to talk about it.

Especially if a pet dies or is hit by a car, and they come home from school and their pet is gone and no one seems to be talking about their pet.

There are many children who have grown up with these words: "No one is allowed to talk about the death. If you do, you may cause pain and hurt to your mother/father, grandparents and cause them to be very sad as well." Therefore, there is no communication within the family circle and sadness is occurring, but the children don't know why and might even think it is their fault that the family is so sad.

So, now who do the children go to for help when trying to figure out what they are feeling inside of them because grandma or grandpa have stopped coming by to see them---- the child/teen may be thinking maybe they are not coming by because of something they may have said or done?

When nothing is said, it is very possible that the child/teen could hear about this death from a friend at school, a neighbor or even someone who they see in the store who offers their sympathies to the family and the child hears this and asks what happened to grandma/grandpa?

Some well-meaning adult might say something like; "Fred sure looked like he was sleeping peacefully in that casket," which could cause a child who hears that to be afraid to go to sleep because they might die too. Another person might say, "she was sick and going to die anyway, she is with the angels now." When the child gets sick, they may think they are going to die too.

Remember the imaginations of children can go in many different directions. Children often take everything they hear very literal. If the child or teen goes to church or Sunday school and hears someone say, "it was God's Will Mary died," That could really cause confusion in the mind of a child/teen or at times even an adult.

The key to talking with children when a death occurs is to answer their questions by being honest. Don't make it sound like a fairy tale, where they live happily ever after. Don't say someone passed----but rather that they died and explain what that means, such as they stop breathing, etc.

If the child is very young, answer in small amounts. Remember their attention span is very short and they can only understand so much at one time.

It is also important to speak on the child's level so they can understand what the adult is trying to tell them. They don't need technical terms, just simple comforting words and perhaps a hug to help them understand what has happened.

If they seem to be afraid or confused that they will die or you will die, it is very important to reassure them they are okay and so are you.

The more the child/teen is told the better off they will be as they get older and have to deal with other deaths in their lives. The more they hear from you, the more they will believe and trust you with their sadness and fears.

On those days when you are having a hard time with your own grief as an adult and perhaps crying, your child /teen maybe the one who comforts you because they know why you are sad and they miss the deceased person too. It is okay to share your grief, that gives the child permission to feel what they feel without feeling they are upsetting you because they too are sad about the death.

It is important to notify their teachers and the school counselor that a death has occurred so they can watch for any changes of behavior in the child/teen or changes in their school work and then they can alert you and make you aware of how the child/teen might be responding to the death.

If you decide to take them to the visitation, funeral or cemetery, be sure to ask them if they want to go; if they don't, please don't force them to go and make plans to have them stay with one of their friends or a relative.

However, if they say yes, then explain to them what, they might see and hear at the visitation, funeral or cemetery, so they will know what to expect. It is also important to go a little early so you and they can have some private time with your deceased loved one before everyone arrives.

If they want to leave, then try to have a plan in place that they can go to a friend's home or a relative's home where they can play and not be alone.

There are some funeral homes that have supervised play areas in the funeral home in the back or tables where the child can color or read while the visitation is going on. A good thing to check on when making arrangements.

So, again the answer to should a child or teen be told when a death occurs, the answer is YES.

WHO ARE THE FORGOTTEN SURVIVORS?

When a death occurs in a family, who are usually the last ones to be told? They are usually the forgotten survivors----the children/teens and sometimes the grandparents. This may sound strange to you, but if you think about It, you will realize it is true. So, your question may be why does that often happen?

Here are several possible answers:

1. The adults are having a very hard time dealing with the death and it is just too difficult to try to tell the children/teens-grandparents right now.
2. The adults are very protective of their children as well as the grandparents and don't want to upset them.
3. Adults often think children are resilient and will get over this loss quickly, so it is ok to tell them later.

4. It is better not to upset the children/teens or grandparents because it will be too painful for them so let's not talk about the death when they are around.

These are answers that might make sense, but is it really fair to the forgotten survivors to not tell them of the death? How do you explain your tears? How do you explain your change of emotions when they are around? How do you explain the absence of the person or pet that is no longer around?

Children/teens and even grandparents need to know who has died, whether it is a parent, another grandparent, a friend of the family, a friend of the child or teen, a teacher, or even their pet.

I realize this is very difficult to do, but just taking the time to talk and listen to them could help them as well as you. If they know you are crying or sad because someone died, this gives them permission to cry with you and comfort you as you comfort them.

It is better to hear from you rather than from a neighbor or someone at school, because they may not understand why you didn't tell them.

If a death is not discussed in the home, then what happens when the child or teen gets a little older and another death occurs? Who can they trust with their feelings? What do they do with how they are feeling inside. Do they become scared or angry every time there is a death, because they don't know what to do or where to go for help when they are sad.

Young children may become inward, or cry a lot, want to be alone, suck their thumb, wet their bed, or become antagonistic toward friends or even the teacher or other children at school.

A teen's grades may drop, they may search for an outlet other than their family to deal with their emotions such as drugs, drinking or possibly even cutting themselves.

These forgotten survivors can navigate through their losses, if someone will only take the time to sit and talk and listen to their pain. This can be a difficult process to go through for the adult as well as the child/teen but in the long run it will help everyone involved.

If after a few weeks the child/teen seems to be struggling with the death, perhaps a grief support group for children or teens would help. They will be able to connect with others that are struggling and can get the help they may need at the time. Hospitals, churches and even funeral homes may have a program or can perhaps direct you to a group or someone who can help them as well as you.

It is also very important to contact the school, the teacher, school counselor as well as the school nurse. This way they can be aware of any sudden changes that may take place in the child/teen and the reasons for their change in attitude or behavior. This will allow them to take care of the situation by talking and listening to the child/teen and letting them know they care about them and are there for them if they need to talk.

Think about it, the last time your family experienced a death, how was it handled and were the forgotten survivors included and if not, then why not? If they were included and you spent time talking and listening to them, Blessings to you!!!

Congratulations and THANK YOU for not allowing those often forgotten to be forgotten!!!!! If not, perhaps you may have some difficult work ahead of you in the future.

WHAT DO ADOLESCENTS WANT FROM US WHEN THEY ARE EXPERIENCING A DIFFICULT TIME IN THEIR LIVES?

Adolescense is a very difficult time in a young person's life, yet they all seemed to struggle through it one way or another. These young men and women are at a stage in their lives, where they are trying to figure out who they are, where they are, what they want to do in their life, are they going to college, trade school, no school, get a job and make some money and perhaps get more education in the future, etc.

As adults, what can we possibly do to help them at this very difficult time in their lives? What do they want from us and what do they need from us?

The answer is simple but sometimes we get so frustrated with them and they with us, that there seems to be a break down in communicating with them and them with us. This is also a time when cars are fast and no one can tell them what to do, especially when drugs or alcohol is available and they could be around it. This is a time when some young people lose their lives from car accidents, drug overdoses, too much alcohol. This is also the time when the media, phones and girl/boy relationships are becoming more and more.

This is also a time for families to think before they speak, listen to their teens with an open heart and to practice patience as hard as that may be for everyone involved. This is a time to listen to them and allow them to talk and communicate their feelings and thoughts not the time to judge them. This is the time to show you trust them and that they can come to you with anything they want to talk about and you will be there to listen and support them and not judge them.

What they need and want from us is simply to Listen to them and support them as they try to figure out what they are thinking about and helping them to figure out who they are. As all of you know this is a difficult time for teens as well as families.

Parents and Grandparents want the best for their children and grandchildren and would do anything they could to help them, whether it is financially or giving them advice as to what they should pursue in their life, how to act, helping them find a job, trying to fix their problems as well as trying to protect them from the world around them and keep them from abusing drugs and alcohol.

The media and the computer and some of their friends can sometimes have a lot to do with how they might be thinking. Remember, this is a time when teens talk a lot with each other, get together and trust what they are saying, and often families are left out.

These are all wonderful things for them to do, but at the same time, they need to be listened to as well as supported. However, what if they were to tell their families what they were really interested in pursuing and the family was disappointed in their choice, because they had plans for them such as perhaps, following in their footsteps and being the success they have become by hard work.

How does the teen interpret their suggestions? The teen could agree and pursue their suggestion, or pursue what they truly believe is the way for them to go. Remember, the adolescent wants to be heard and not told what to do, even though it might be a wonderful idea for the adolescent.

This could cause a break down in communication between the adolescent and the family and possibly a time when the adolescent doesn't feel they can trust the family with their ideas without getting unsolicitous advice and therefore doesn't share their ideas and thoughts with their family.

However, this could also be a time for trust and communicating with everyone involved and a chance to share ideas, thoughts and feelings of trust.

When a sudden death occurs in their lives such as a suicide, car accident, or an over dose of drugs or alcohol, who can they go to for support? When their grades are dropping or they are skipping classes for whatever reason, who can they turn to for support?

The answer is simply to give them what they want which is to be heard and supported. They need to be able to come to parents and grandparents and know that whatever is happening in their young life, that they are being heard, supported and not judged.

No one ever said adolescence was an easy time in their lives or the families.

In reality, this a form of grief, which may sound strange, but is it? Think about when a death occurs: there often is confusion, not being able to focus, needing support, needing someone to depend on to help you get through this difficult time. A time to talk and a time to be heard, to express how you feel, without being told how you should feel. Trusting that there is someone there who can help you through this difficult time. A time when it is okay not to be okay.

Adolescence can be the same way at times. Blessings to those of you who are parents, grandparents, friends, teachers, counselors as you help our adolescences to navigate through these difficult times.

TIPS FOR PARENTS WHEN THERE HAS BEEN A DEATH

When there has been a death, as a parent, grandparent or guardian, what do you say to your children? How do you reach out to them?

Here are some tips that could help with what you say to them and what you can expect from them. The age of the child is very important and will make a big difference in what they understand and how they will respond to what you are saying to them.

A preschool child has very little understanding of death and to them everything is temporary and is reversible—like the road runner who gets knocked down over and over again but seems to always come back. This is a time of magical thinking for them that nothing is real and everything is ok.

Preschoolers use their behavior to explain how they feel. They have a fear of being abandoned or left alone, so they may become very clinging, withdrawn, wet their beds, revert back to thumb sucking and even at times become whiny.

This is a time for patience, understanding, and reassurance that mom and dad are ok and will be there with them. When you go to the funeral don't force them to go, if they want to go, please explain briefly what they will see before they get there and be available to them if they need to go home. It is a good idea to go early so they can experience what you told them before everyone arrives for the actual visitation or funeral.

They also love to play and their attention span is very short, so they may go outside and play and come back in, ask you a question and then go out again back and forth.

The child who is between five and nine, usually has an understanding that death is not reversible and that death can happen to anyone. They often think of death as a monster who comes to get you. They need to spend more time with family before bedtime, because they often associate death with darkness.

These children will want a detailed account of what happened to the person who died. They need honest and direct answers, not technical answers. Please respect their decision to go or not go to the visitation or funeral as well as the cemetery. These children should be told ahead of time what they will see at the funeral home or the church for the visitation and funeral before they actually go to either service.

It is very important for their teachers and school counselors to know that there has been a death and to perhaps keep an eye on them. This age has a tendency to become very aggressive toward their teachers, other students such as throwing things, yelling out and can be very disruptive in the class so as to get the attention that they may not be getting at home because everyone is grieving.

Remember, sometimes any kind of attention is okay even if it means they are in trouble, because at least someone is paying special attention to them.

If possible, ask if there is a place for children to sit and read or color or play games at the funeral home. If there is something for children, you might let them bring their favorite coloring book or even their favorite stuffed animal to hold on to.

Preteen children are caught in between childhood and adolescence and often not sure what to do with that. They know that death is final and that everyone will die sometime. They may cry, but feel embarrassed about it and not cry in front of anyone. They need to know it is okay to feel what they feel.

Please explain to them that they may feel different emotions at different times and that is okay, such as sudden burst of anger, tears, sadness and even feel very lonely and may with draw from their friends.

They too need to know what they will see and hear at the visitation, funeral and cemetery. Some may be crying others may be laughing still others just being very quiet. They also may want to look in the casket and touch the person, explain about what they will see and feel before they go.

Always leave the door open to listen!! Never say their loved one looks like they are sleeping, because they may be afraid to go to sleep because they too may die.

Be sure that their teachers and school counselors are aware there has been a death, so they can keep an eye on the child just in case they begin to act differently then they normally do.

Teenagers, are caught between childhood and adulthood. They may act like they have everything together, but inside they really don't. They live for the moment and don't feel death will happen to them, but perhaps to someone else. They like to take risks and don't always care about the consequences.

It is also very important that their teachers and school counselors are aware that there has been a death and to keep an eye on the teen, especially if they suddenly become moody, grades begin to drop and they become a bit "mouthy."

They may experience stomachaches, headaches, a decreased or increase in their appetite, have trouble sleeping, may withdraw and become even more sensitive than they usually are.

They may feel guilty, and even think about ending their life, because they blame themselves for the person's death because they had an argument or yelled at them, and the person died a couple days later.

WHAT HELPS?? Listening to them and being patient with them. They love to listen to music, they like to express their feelings by being active such as: writing songs in memory of their loved one who died, art work, help mom or dad get through their sadness, hang out with their friends, write poems and be of help when possible.

Parents remember, grandparents grieve twice. Once for your loss and once for their loved one. So, be kind to them as well as your children and most of all be kind and patient with yourself. Blessing to all of you!!!!!

HAVE YOU EVER HAD A LOVED ONE WHO ENDED THEIR LIFE?

Does depression always lead to suicide? Does suicide always come from someone who is depressed? The answer to both of these questions is NO.

However, it seems that in January and February many teens and adults become depressed or end their lives. Several years ago, John Hewett the author of "After Suicide" wrote, "that a loved one's death by suicide leaves the survivors with a triple whammy. First, someone close has died; second, the death was sudden; third, one has to deal with the additional pain and regret of suicide."

He is correct on all three accounts. I have written two books on grief "Comforting the Bereaved Through Listening and Positive Responding, sub title, (What are the Bereaved Trying to Tell Us?)" and "Signs or Coincidences subtitle (What are the Deceased Trying to Tell Us?)" where suicide and depression are both discussed.

Those left behind do deal with a lot of pain, guilt, anger, sadness, blame, bewilderment as well as many other feelings. Often the survivors blame themselves and deal with the "should haves and could haves," thinking they should have or could have prevented this suicide.

However, the truth is: a person only ends their life for two reasons: one reason, they are hurting so bad (mentally, physically, socially, spiritually, emotionally), it really makes no difference. The pain is so severe that they cannot deal with it anymore. The second reason, is that they have lost hope. Once these feelings come together there is no turning back and no way to stop it. If by chance they are interrupted when trying to end their life, they may stop but continue another time and succeed next time.

You see if there is still some kind of hope left, no matter how small, they will not end their life because there is that chance, that just maybe they can get the help they need. However, many families and friends are not aware of this and blame themselves over and over again when really there was nothing they could have done.

Often times January and February are thought of as depression and suicide months, because of the holidays they experienced or didn't experience and the feelings of being let down that lingers on and on after the holidays are over.

Occasionally, children/teens and even older people are left to deal with their pain or possible depression alone or their family may think they are okay and they go on with life thinking everything is okay when in reality it definitely isn't.

Suicide is often completed in solitude, however, there are some that want someone to witness their suicide for reasons of revenge. There are also accidental suicides due to abuse of drugs or alcohol with their friends who end their lives.

However, usually the person who ends their life has a plan and does not want anyone around. Their plan usually makes certain that no one is around to stop them, interrupt them or watch them end their life.

Often there is no note left behind to explain what the survivors want to know, which is "WHY." If a note is left behind it is usually to ask for forgiveness or to say their good byes.

If you were to look back in the deceased' life you can often find a map of what they have been experiencing for many years, but yet, others may not always recognize the symptoms or may think they will grow out these feelings.

Suicide does not just happen, there are circumstances that the person has accumulated over the years and now see no way out of their pain.

They may experience feelings of hopelessness, pain, despair, and possible severe depression. Sometimes the breakup of a relationship, poor grades in school, putting unrealistic expectations on themselves and failing to be able to meet those expectations in sports, or life itself.

Sometimes even body image can cause them to want to end their life, because they feel they are too thin or over weight (and when in reality they are not either) but they are bullied on line or at school and tend to believe what they hear and read and decide to end their life.

Those that are older often deal with the thoughts of suicide, due to becoming very lonely and feeling no one cares about them anymore. Many of their friends have already died and they may feel that they have been forgotten or just lonely and miss their friends and someone to talk to, especially since no one comes to visit or call them like they used too.

It is very important to keep in touch by calling or visiting with someone who is older as often as you can and invite them to family gatherings as often as possible. It means more than you can imagine to hear from family or friends when you are feeling lonely and thinking that no one cares about you and there is really no reason to go on living.

Usually, most people are able to deal with difficult thoughts and move on or else get help, but others take these feelings to heart, and they start to believe what others have said and feel like a failure, a burden to others, useless and hopeless.

They may turn to drugs or alcohol for help but find this doesn't work either, the pain is still there. In their minds, the only way to end this pain is to end their life and get the freedom and relief they are looking for.

If you have had someone end their life, please be patient and gentle with yourself. Don't put expectations on yourself and don't allow society, friends or family to put their expectations on you as to your loved ones' death was your fault, because it wasn't. There was nothing you could have done to prevent their death.

Your grief will take a long time to get through and to ease the pain of what you are feeling inside.

It is important to get help: talking to an individual grief therapist or joining an SOS group (a suicide group for family and friends of those that have already ended their lives) can really help.

If you need help, seek it, don't be ashamed or afraid to ask for help. It is very important for you to talk to someone professionally so you can get the help you need. Your life has been changed drastically by a suicide and your feelings and thoughts are not the same as other types of losses.

Remember, Grief takes long as it takes, so take as long as you need.

Remember, no two people grieve alike, even men and women grieve differently. If your spouse is grieving differently than you—it is okay.

Don't, try to rush through your grief—no matter what anyone says. Please don't run away from your loss, if you do, grief will wait for you and when you least expect it will appear.

Take one day at a time or one hour at a time. Don't put expectations on yourself. It is okay not to be okay all the time.

Try to eat, rest, and get a little exercise to help you to keep going, because grief can be very tiring and very trying.

Take care of yourself the best you can and remember you are not alone in your grief.

TALKING TO ADOLESCENTS ABOUT SUICIDE

Suicide is often a taboo topic that parents don't want to talk about with their teens because of the fear that perhaps they might end their own life when things get tough for them.

Possible reasons for ending their lives could be: breaking up with their girlfriend/boyfriend, poor grades, not making the cheer leading squad or the athletic team, putting expectations on themselves and then not being able to fulfill them, thinking they are too thin or overweight, when in reality (they are not), trying to get back at someone because they were embarrassed in front of their girlfriend/boyfriend, or abuse of drugs or alcohol. The reasons can go on and on. Some of the reasons may sound silly to adults, but to teenagers, they are very serious.

Suicide rates among teenagers seems to continue to rise year after year. Some may be disguised as an accident, or drug overdose or even not mentioned by families due to the stigma society has put on it. As parents, it is very important to talk to your teen now before a suicide happens as well as after one has happened.

What should you be aware of? Being bullied on-line by another student. Cluster suicides-one person ends their life then another follows suit, then another and another. Falling grades-failing grades, breakup between their boyfriend/girlfriend. When your teen hears about a suicide whether it is at school or even if it is a celebrity and they want to talk—please be available to listen.

A sudden change in their emotions, such as sadness, anger, revenge, their language such as: "You would be better off without me being around," "I am not any good to anyone," "No nobody likes me – I am so dumb." They seem to be in some kind of emotional pain. Listen to them and their words.

They may begin to give away their favorite clothes, books, posters, old tapes to their friends, when these things are very important to them. This is a cry for help—so please be aware.

They may be feeling hopeless and lost. This is not the time to judge or lecture to them but rather to Listen to them as to why they feel this way.

If your teen or any teen has a plan, this is a sign they plan to go through with how they are feeling and may very well try to end their life.

They may be feeling helpless, hopeless, withdrawn from families, friends or even school activities that they loved being involved in. However, they may seem to be very involved with others who have attempted a suicide and failed but really interested in what they tried to do or perhaps have started cutting themselves. Listen and pay attention to their actions as well as their words and perhaps it could be time for someone to intervene and seek out the suicide hotline or other kinds of help.

A person ends their life, no matter what their age is, because of the pain they could be feeling physically, mentally, socially or spiritually and because they have lost hope. Both of these go together. Be aware if any of these signs are prevalent with your teen, please get help for them.

Talk with them---Listen to them---Listen to their joys and their pains. Let them Always know they can come to you about anything anytime. This has to be their time, not just your time. Make time for them—set up a time and be there. Listen to them with your heart not you head. Don't judge them. Try to understand them as hard as that may be for you.

If they are an athlete, be sure to attend their games—don't say you will be there and time after time you are not there. These games are important to them and when you show up to watch them play or the team play, it means more to them than you could ever know. They may not say anything to you, especially if they lose—then they really need you there to encourage them for the next game.

Remember a teenager is all about themselves and trying to learn about life one way or another. Be aware of warning signs.

Be aware of you teenager's friends, especially those who may have attempted a suicide or who are on drugs or alcohol.

A good time to talk with teens is when they are shooting baskets are throwing a football around or hitting golf balls or hiking or camping or cooking, whatever they enjoy doing.

Both of you can relax and just enjoy each other and yet talk and learn a lot about each other.

So, don't panic, but rather Listen with your heart and not you head. And relax and enjoy each other as you get to really know your teenager and they get to know and trust you a little more.

DO YOU THINK YOU MIGHT NEED TO TALK WITH SOMEONE SINCE YOUR LOVED ONE DIED?

Experiencing a loss can be very difficult and painful for many people. The way you are able to navigate or not navigate through your grief can make a big difference in your everyday living.

However, because we live in a death denying society, some people may feel very uncomfortable being around someone who is grieving or someone who is having a difficult time with their loss. There are many unknowing people who tell the bereaved to "Move ON," "Get Over IT," "You'll be 0kAY," (How do they know?), "He/she was old or sick and they were going to die anyway." The problem with this advice is not to comfort the bereaved, but rather to help make the person who is saying this to feel more comfortable, because they cannot understand the true feelings of the bereaved.

Here are some questions you might want to think about and ask yourself if this sounds like where you might be right now. Always remember, Grief takes as long as it takes, there are no time limits and no quick fixes.

However, it is a good idea to have someone to talk with now and then whether it is a grief therapist, a grief group, or a trusted friend, who will listen, not judge you or give you unsolicitous advice.

Questions:
1. Do you seem to be irritable, anxious, angry or feel guilty since your loved one died?
2. Do you feel you have no one to talk with or do you feel isolated from everyone?
3. Do you think you should have done more for your deceased loved one, even though you were with them 24/7?
4. Do you constantly worry about your own death or perhaps someone in your family dying?
5. Are you afraid to meet new people because you feel you might become close to them and then they will die too?
6. Are you unable to focus or concentrate most of the time? Do you try to relax and read a book and read the same sentence over and over again?
7. Are you trying to stay overly busy, in hopes that you will not think about your deceased loved one?
8. Do you feel no one calls you anymore or wants to be around you because you are crying a lot or can't stop talking or thinking about your deceased loved one?

9. Have you cut yourself off from your family and friends?
10. Do you feel guilty, depressed, sad and want to be with your deceased loved one?
11. Do you feel stuck in your grief or that you might be going crazy or out of control?
12. Do you think you are grieving wrong, and can't seem to find the right way?

Remember, it is ok to ask for help!!! It is okay to cry in front of others or alone. It is ok to remember your deceased loved one and talk with them. It is okay to allow others to grieve with you.

When your loved one died, you became part of a New Normal. This simply means, what you feel, think, and do are normal for now. You are NOT going CRAZY, you are Grieving!! This time in your life will pass!! Blessing to you as you navigate through your grief.

WHY DO WE NEED SUPPORT WHEN WE ARE GRIEVING?

This title may sound a bit strange, but in reality, there are many bereaved who are afraid to ask for help because they don't want to be a burden. There are still others who feel they can grieve on their own, because everyone has told them they are strong and will "get over this." Really?? There is a wonderful saying from William Shakespeare, "Everyone can master a grief but he that has it." I think William Shakespeare was right on target.

Because people who have not experienced a death, have no idea the pain that is involved in losing someone dear to them. It also very uncomfortable for those who have never experienced a loss to see their friend or colleague going through this "New Normal" that the bereaved are experiencing.

I think many of the non- bereaved in their own way, want to help but are not sure what to say or do and often come out with hurtful words for their family member, friend or colleague.

So, why do the bereaved need support to help them get through their loss? It is very important for the bereaved to feel free to talk with someone they trust and share their feelings and their story, without having someone telling them, "I liked you the way you used to be, when you were happy and smiling, not crying all the time." "What is wrong with you?"

It is in the telling of your story that your healing takes place. In other words, when we bury out thoughts and feelings so deep inside of us that we are afraid to reach out to someone or even a grief group, our healing seems to take a lot longer to get through.

It is very important to feel what you feel and allow others to reach out to you as you reach out to them. For example, if your children see you crying and try to comfort you and you tell them you are fine or okay, they may be afraid to cry in front of you or show you their feelings and keep their feelings inside of them, because they don't want to upset you. When you allow others to see you cry, that gives them permission to comfort you or even cry with you and not be afraid that you will be upset by their tears.

Some people feel if they cry, they are weak—not true. When you allow yourself to love someone, you risk the chance of crying. Crying is just another form of love for your deceased loved one.

When we experience a loss, we lose all control. It is time to take some of that control back and tell people what you want from them. If you don't tell people what you need from them, they don't know how to respond to you and they go away very confused.

It is also important to remember that Grief takes as long as it takes, there is no time limit. Everyone grieves differently so, don't put expectations on yourself to move on, there are plenty of others who will do that for you.

Often people question their faith and stop going to church or blame God for their loss. This is really not unusual. However, it might be a good idea to reach out to the clergy or someone you feel comfortable with to talk about how you are feeling. It is nothing to be ashamed of, it is often a normal reaction to a death.

Please do not beat yourself up and feel something is wrong with you, because this is simply grief trying to take over. Remember, grief can affect you in many ways.

When someone is grieving, they often are unable to focus, to think, often feel a deep sadness, very fatigued, have aches and pains in their body, lose friends, feel guilty or angry, have trouble eating or sleeping, have no motivation to do anything and have doubts about their faith. These are normal responds to loss and grief, it doesn't mean someone is grieving wrong if they feel any of these things, it is just what grief can do to us when a loved one dies.

This is why it is so important to have some kind of support when grieving, so you are not alone, but rather know you have the support of others to help you get through this difficult time in your life.

Remember, there is no right way or wrong way to grieve, only the way that works for you. If it isn't working than you need to think about what helped you in the past, when you were having a difficult time.

Perhaps following that path or reaching out to a grief group, grief therapist or close trusted friend who will listen and not give you unsolicitous advice is the path to follow.

It is also very important to reach out to your doctor and have a checkup several months after a death just to see how you are doing. But be sure to tell them you have experienced a death and that is why you are feeling the way you are at this time. If you do need medication, please be very aware that they do not give you too much medication that you cannot function at all.

In conclusion: Blessings to all of you. Please take care of yourself and let others in to help support you and walk with you as you navigate through your loss. Always remember: Mt. 5:4 "Blessed are those who mourn for they shall be comforted."

WHAT IS A GRIEF SUPPORT GROUP?

That might seem like a strange question, but is it really? A grief support group is to help someone who is grieving. True!!! But there are many different kinds of grief groups such as for a death, divorce, suicide, children/teens, death of a pet, a SHARE group, SIDS, baby, cancer, stroke, the list goes on and on.

How do you know which group you should go to? How soon should you start looking for a group? Who should go? Is there a certain age limit? Can you take someone with you for support? Does it cost to go to one? Once you find one, how do you know it is the right one for you? Where do I look for a grief group? These are just a few questions that many people struggle with when they are in need of help.

I facilitate three grief groups at the hospital where I am a chaplain. A SOS group (a suicide group for friends and families of those who have already ended their lives), another grief group for everything except suicide and we just started a children/teen grief group for ages 5 to 18 years of age for those who experienced a loss from death everything from a pet to parents, grandparents, siblings, friends etc.

It is important to perhaps start looking after two or three months after a death for some help if you feel you may need it, whether it is a group or individual, that of course is up to the bereaved.

Often the family feels the bereaved person needs to have help now—that however, is not always true. It is very important for the bereaved to be with family and friends at the beginning to comfort them, listen to them and help them deal with death certificates, burial, thank you cards, etc.

The problem that often occurs, if they do go too early to a group or individual counseling, the bereaved individual is in so much pain and shock, that they cannot comprehend what is being said in the group or individual counseling and often leave and do not return because they feel they were not helped; when in reality, they were not truly ready in their own mind that they may need help and they were only following the advice of someone telling them they should seek help.

If the bereaved person goes to individual counseling, they should be sure there is a connection between the therapist and their self and that they feel they are being listened to and helped. If this doesn't occur, they should find someone else. If it is grief from a death, divorce, health related they need to find someone in that area, not just a therapist, but rather someone who specializes in that field.

If a couple's baby just died, they need to be sure this is the correct group or individual to help them. Some suggestions: for the death of a baby is a SHARE, or a SIDS group (depending on the type of death); a child/teen- Bereaved Parents group. If it is a divorce- a divorce group not just a grief group but rather one specializing in Divorce.

Who should go to a group? Anyone who wants to be around others who have perhaps experienced a similar death and they can relate to. Remember, however groups are not for everyone. It is always a good idea to ask the person in charge if they can bring someone with them for the first couple of times. This might give the bereaved some strength if someone is allowed to be there with them at first and someone they can talk with later.

Always ask if there is a cost for the group sessions, better to ask before you decide to go than to go unprepared. There usually isn't a cost, but it is always good to ask.

Where do you look for groups? The best thing to do is to call the hospitals (Pastoral Care) nearby, the funeral homes, churches, or ask your physician or nurses and your friends who have attended a group before. Most hospitals, funeral homes and churches usually have a list of what is available or can direct you to the correct place to get the information you are seeking.

Is there an age limit to go to a group or individual therapist? No, but usually children/teens are not allowed in adult groups. So, it is important to seek out a grief group for children and teens, so that they too can get the help they may be needing.

Remember, you are not alone in your grief, there is someone there who can listen, comfort you and help you. Just be sure you look when you are ready and not when someone tells you they think you need help.

DO YOU LISTEN TO WHAT YOUR DOG IS TRYING TO TELL YOU? DO YOU UNDERSTAND THEIR SIGNALS?

Now that spring is here and summer is just around the corner, everyone seems to be out walking their dog. However, not all dogs are interested in being socialized. Many are scared when another dog or human approaches them.

For example, when a dog comes over to sniff you, it doesn't necessarily mean they want you to pet them. It simple means they are sniffing you, to see who you are, where you have been and perhaps who you have been with. It does not mean they want you to get down on their level and pet them----they might see it as being aggressive toward them.

It is important to be aware of their language before you step in or allow your child to step in and try to pet the dog without their permission. It is important to learn how to communicate with them before you make an innocent mistake and someone gets hurt.

According to Tufts University -Cummings School of Veterinary Medicine, there are three communication signals to be aware of: Scratching -sneezing and yawning, closed -fist, and tail wagging.

The first signal: scratching or sneezing could certainly mean they feel itchy or sneezy but when they suddenly get down and start scratching it could also mean they are trying to avoid contact with you. Yawning is also a clue that they are feeling tension or feeling uncomfortable with the situation.

The second signal the closed fist: putting your closed fist in front of their nose, might seem like you are doing the right thing to get the attention of the dog or that you are friendly and just want to pet them— a very innocent jester in your mind, however not in theirs. They may however, feel very uncomfortable with a fist in front of them and think of it as an aggressive signal to them to be on their guard. They may back up from you or move their head away from you. If this happens, they are trying to tell you, they don't want you to touch them. Remember, not every dog wants to have a stranger pet them.

The third signal tail wagging: Is not always a sign that they are happy. Look for these signs, "While their tail is wagging. Is their body carriage stiff, ridged? Are their ears pinned back? Do they have a fixed stare, or are their eyes blinking rapidly? Is their mouth pulled back tight with the teeth showing, "listen to the teeth not the tail?" "A rigid stance means the dog is ready to fight, while pinned-back ears and rapid blinking indicates anxiety, and a fixed stare signals either aggression or fear that can lead to aggression."

However, it is also possible if the dog's body is calm and it seems as though their eyes are happy and relaxed, it is okay to pet the dog because in this case a wagging tail is a good sign. Also, if their teeth are not showing while their tail is wagging, that is another good sign.

Did you know that a dog has to learn that a hug is good? Young children try to hug dogs (whether they know them or not). However, putting your arm over them is a sign of dominance. Again, be aware of what you are doing when approaching a dog.

So, enjoy your walk, but don't be so quick to approach a dog or allow your child to either, without checking out the signals. In fact, another idea is to ask the owner of the dog if their dog bites and if they are ok with you or your child petting their dog, this could save a lot of embarrassment as well as distress for the dog, the owner and you and your family.

Remember your words and actions can make a difference, so be careful what you do and what you say.

WHAT SHOULD YOU SAY TO SOMEONE WHOSE PET HAS DIED?

Just like any kind of a death, the death of a pet can be very difficult. Pet owners grieve just like anybody else when a death happens. There are certain things you should not say to someone when a loved one (human) dies and there are certain words you should not say when a pet dies.

According to Tufts University – Cummings School of Veterinary Medicine there are certain words that should not be said to a grieving pet owner.

Let's take a quiz……. Which example would you choose to say to someone who is grieving? 1) He's/ she's not suffering anymore. 2) At least you got to have him/her for as long as you did. 3) You gave him/her a good life. 4) Give it some time. 5) Better not to say any of these. 6) All of the above are good, comforting things to say.

What did you choose? The correct answer is 5. Truthfully, none of these answers should be said to anyone who is grieving except for number 5, because the intent can seem to them that you are telling them how they should be feeling due do this death and not really giving them comfort, but only making matters worse.

For example, if you were to tell someone their pet or human loved one, lived a long life, that certainly doesn't help their grief, because it is never a good time to have someone die, no matter how long they have lived.

The best thing someone can do for the bereaved person is to acknowledge their emotional pain rather than telling them something you may regret later. Death is very difficult and sad for anyone whether their loved one died or their beloved pet died. Telling someone they can always get another one it was only an animal, is also a terrible thing to say to someone grieving a pet.

So, what should you say to a grieving pet owner? Tufts University Cummings School of Veterinary Medicine recommends these: 1) "I am so very sorry for your loss". 2) "I wish there were words that could help." 3) "I miss him, too. I love how he used to (insert "jump on the couch;" "steal food," "play with his toys," etc.) 4) "If you need anything, I am here." (Be sure you are, if you say that to someone). 5) "I know how much you loved him/her." And the last one, 6) "Don't talk. Just hug, or simply sit with the person." If you give someone a hug, please remember to ask them if it is ok if you give them a hug. There are some people who do not want a hug from anyone.

Those are just a few things that can be said to a pet owner There are many more words that can be shared. Just THINK before you speak. What would you want someone to say to you, if your pet died? Please remember, these pets who have died are a big part of their family, so don't make light of this loss.

It is also a good idea to perhaps bring a meal over to the family or something that might bring them comfort. The things you do for the bereaved whether it due to the death of a human loved one or a pet loved one is appreciated and means a lot to the bereaved that you cared enough to take the time to acknowledge their loss.

Tufts University Cummings School of Veterinary Medicine: www.tuftsyourdog.com

PETS GRIEVE TOO!

We know that most people grieve the death of a pet, but do animals grieve the loss of their human companion or another animal in the house? What about their friend next store? What about birds, elephants, and other animals as well? The answer is yes. Animals grieve the loss of their own as well as others.

The most obvious signs of pet grief are a loss of appetite, withdrawal, frequent revisiting of places that had meaning for them. Pets may also show grief by sitting by or on a chair where their deceased owner always sat, or by returning to the deceased owners' gravesite after weeks or months have passed. They are also known to cling to the bereaved to help them care for and support them in their grief.

Animals may also grieve the death of other animals. The American Society for the Prevention of Cruelty to Animals (ASPCA) in 1996 conducted a survey to gauge the degree of pet responses to the death of another pet. The survey included observations about eating habits, vocalizations, solicitations of affection, and other activities after the death of a "sibling" animal. Responses showed that more than a third of the dogs in the survey demanded more attention and 25 percent were described as "needy" or "clingy."

The responses for cats were slightly different with almost 40 percent needing more attention, and only 20 percent were characterized as being "clingy" or "needy." Grieving cats are still cats.

Another typical response of a grieving pet is a change in appetite for several days up to months at a time. The conclusion of the survey was that, yes, pets show signs of grief. It has also been proven that not only dogs and cats grieve, but ducks, horses, elephants and birds as well.

Even in the wild, birds show their grief. One day, I was sitting on my sofa when I heard a loud bang on my patio window. I looked up saw a female tufted titmouse bird had flown into the window and was lying on the deck. Within minutes, a male tufted titmouse bird came to her rescue. He began to peck and peck at her as if trying to revive her, but to no avail. A smaller bird appeared, but he chased it away. The male bird then continued to try to revive her until he realized it was hopeless, at which point he laid his little body and head against the female for several minutes and then flew away. It was very sad, but a beautiful example of an animal showing his love and grief over the death of a loved one.

Remember, if you ever suspect your pet is grieving, be sure to give them that extra attention and unconditional love they so deserve. The words you say and the actions you take do matter.

Thanks, and Blessings to all of you who take the time to acknowledge this difficult loss.

The American Society for the Prevention of Cruelty to Animals: 424 E. 92ndSt New York, NY 10128-6804

THE HOLIDAYS AND SOME IDEAS ON HOW TO GET THROUGH THEM

One of the many issues facing the bereaved every year are the holidays, anniversaries and birthdays and how to survive them, especially if they are newly bereaved.

It seems when we are near a holiday, there is usually an anniversary or birthday right around the corner. These holidays seem to start with Halloween, then Thanksgiving, Advent, Christmas, Hanukkah, Kwanzaa, New Years Eve, New Years Day, Valentines Day and many others. It seems to go on and on.

Between the grocery stores, department stores, media, music in the stores, flowers, hearts, candles, indoor and outdoor decorations etc. it is very hard to escape. The problem with many of these things, is that they occur months before the actual holiday occurs, which seems to be a constant reminder of what is coming and often panic sets in as to "What am I going to do?" The anticipation of what is coming is often worst for many bereaved than the actual day or holiday.

So, what is the answer? It is simple—have a PLAN. Tradition is wonderful, but sometimes it can wait for a year or two or even change the tradition to meet the situation. For example: if you always have a real Christmas tree, this year either have no tree, or an artificial tree or even decorate a large plant.

Sometimes families try to keep everything the same for the holidays, but it will never be the same, because your loved one will no longer be there to celebrate with you.

Here are some plans that might help you: Instead of having everyone over for the holidays, perhaps this is the year to go out for dinner or instead of hosting everyone at your house, go to someone else's home for dinner.

Instead of you always making everything yourself, have everyone bring their favorite dish or assign everyone a certain thing to bring.

Instead of baking pies, perhaps you could buy one or have someone else bring one or two.

If you should be invited to someone's house for dinner and you think this might be very difficult for you, then you have the option of not going. However, if you should decide to go, if it is not too far away and you might consider driving yourself, that way if you should need to leave early-you can and no one else has to leave with you.

If You should decide to go to someone's house for dinner, it is very important for you to share with your host/hostess, how you are feeling about the holiday and coming over due to your recent loss, especially if you are having a difficult time. Be sure they know that you might have to leave the room for a couple minutes or leave early because you may be feeling overwhelmed with everyone and your loss.

Perhaps you could come over later when there are fewer people and everyone is not trying to make you feel better by their cheerful words, such as "Wishing you the best on this wonderful day," or "If you would smile, you might feel better instead of crying so much."

If you always send cards or Christmas letters, perhaps this is the year to either send none or cut your list down to those you do not see all the time and the next year or the year after you can resume your Christmas card and letter lists.

If you do send cards and letters and want to include your deceased loved one in the card/letter, you can include their name at the bottom where you sign your name but have their name in quotation marks or parenthesis.

The holidays can be emotionally, physically, and psychologically very draining. So, be sure to get plenty of rest and relax when you can over the holidays before, during and after.

If would like to remember your loved one during the holidays, you could light a candle and place it on the counter or table, offer a prayer in remembrance of your loved one, raising a glass and toasting your loved one.

You could also give money to their favorite charity in memory of them. If they loved to read, perhaps dedicate a book to the library in memory of them. All of these ideas could create a chance for others to perhaps share stories, memories and even how they may be feeling.

If you decide to put up a tree, you could also buy a small tree and use it only in memory of your loved one. The only ornaments on the small tree would be ones that remind you of them. Every year add another ornament to this special tree. In fact, others may want to contribute an ornament to this small tree in memory of your loved one.

Instead of shopping in person and attacked by all the elves running around you could simply send gift cards, shop on line or from a catalog. You would be surprised how many good deals you might be able to get.

It is also very important to feel what you feel and not try to mask your feeling for everyone around you. It is okay to cry. It is okay not to be okay.

It may seem that the holidays are going to be terrible, and yes, there could be some difficult times. But it is okay to laugh, smile and enjoy yourself without feeling guilty or that you have forgotten your loved one, or that you have loved them any less.

Remember, anticipating the holidays, a birthday or anniversary is much worse than the actual day. God Bless all of you!!!!!!!!

THE HOILDAYS AND WHY THEY CAN BE DIFFICULT

One of the problems for the bereaved during the holidays is that the holiday season seems to go on and on. The department stores start advertising several months before the actual holiday. For example: have you ever walked into a store in August and seen Halloween costumes or in October and seen Thanksgiving and Christmas items or at the end of December and seen Valentine hearts everywhere you look?

Everyone is looking forward to the holidays, so why aren't we? The answer is simple: a part of us is dead. A part of us is missing. A part of us is empty. When our loved one died or was killed, a part of us died with them. A part that can never be replaced by another child, another spouse, another parent or another sibling. We can never go back to the way we were, because we are not the same person that we used to be.

So, what makes society and advertisers think everyone is ready, willing, and able for the holidays to begin? Because we live in a death dying society, no one wants to talk with or deal with someone who is crying, confused, upset or sad because of a death. Unless you are bereaved or have been bereaved, you may not have a clue as to what someone who is bereaved may be feeling.

When we grieve, we grieve not only the person who has died, but also the life that we have lived and loved with that person. We grieve the happy times, the sad times, the important times and the not so important times that we were together. We also grieve those very special times during the holidays that we were together; those Kodak moments, special rituals, customs and traditions that we shared year after year. All of this is interwoven into the many memories of our loved ones. Just the thought of a first holiday or another holiday without our loved one can be almost unbearable for the bereaved.

Just hearing the sounds of the approaching holidays can bring us to our knees. We may feel disconnected with our family and our friends, but yet we try to be happy when we are really feeling, so empty and alone inside. Sometimes even being in a crowd can be lonely.

We may feel like the nursery rhyme Humpty Dumpty who was in so many pieces they didn't know what to do or how to put him back together again. Perhaps what we need to do, is rearrange those pieces and try to put them back together in a different form. Since, we can't go back, we need to live with what we've got and move forward step by step, day by day, hour by hour. On those rough days, when it is hard to even put one foot in front of the other, we need to find someone to talk to or just spend some time alone and just relax and wait for a better and softer moment to move forward.

Sometimes we run away from our grief by trying to keep busy and very active, so that we don't have to deal with the pain of our loss. The problem with that is, when we do slow down, our grief is there waiting for us to return. So, what can we do to get through the holidays, birthdays, anniversaries and other special occasions?

Here are some suggestions to help you get through the holidays:

BE PATIENT WITH YOURSELF AND THOSE AROUND YOU. DON'T PUT EXPECTATIONS ON YOURSELF OR OTHERS.

HAVE A PLAN OR TWO as to what you might be doing over the holidays and then tell your plan to your friends and family so they know what they might expect from you. If you are invited to do something you'd rather not do, be tentative but honest in giving your answer.

IT IS OKAY TO CHANGE YOUR TRADITION. Perhaps, having Thanksgiving or Christmas dinner at a different house or going out for dinner instead of cooking might be a good change for this year.

COUNTER THE CONSPIRACY OF SILENCE by talking about your loved one. Because your family and friends love you, they may think they are doing you a favor by not mentioning your loved one for fear you will be upset. You can break the silence by mentioning him/her yourself and explain to them how important it is to you to be able to remember your loved one during the holidays. This could invite others to join in and tell a story or memory of your loved one as well.

FIND A CREATIVE OUTLET TO REMEMBER YOUR LOVED ONE. You could write a memorial poem or story about your loved one and share it with others. Use the money that you would have spent for a gift for that special person, to buy something for someone he or she cared about.

CONSIDER CUTTING BACK ON YOUR CARD SENDING. It is not really necessary to send cards to people you will see over the holidays.

HOLIDAYS often magnify feelings of the loss of a loved one. It is important and natural to experience the sadness that comes during the holidays. To try to block those feelings is unhealthy. Please keep the positive memory of your loved one alive and just feel what you feel and don't try to hide it. If you are going to someone's house for dinner, you might explain to them before you get there, that this might be a difficult day for you and you might need to step out for a few minutes. This way they are aware of what could happen.

EMOTIONALLY, PHYSICALLY AND PSYCHOLOGICALLY, THE HOLIDAYS ARE DRAINING. You need every bit of strength and rest you can get.

SOME PEOPLE FEAR crying in public, especially at a church service. However, it is really okay to cry. You should try to be gentle with yourself. If you do cry, you will probably feel better. If you need to get up and leave for a short time, it is okay—perhaps you might even feel better to sit in a different place when you return.

SET LIMITATIONS. Realize, that the holidays are NOT going to be easy. Do the things that are very special and important to you. If you don't feel like shopping this year and being attacked by Santa's elves, then try shopping through the internet or a catalog or just give gift certificates. You could even give a donation to the charity of your choice in memory of your loved one.

YOU might buy a small tree and an ornament for that tree that reminds you of your loved one. Every year add another ornament to this special tree.

Often after the first year, the people in your life may expect you to be "Over it", however, you never "Get Over It," rather you get through your grief. Everyone may expect you to be happy and excited like they are about the holidays and can't seem to understand what is taking you so long. What they don't understand is that, there is no time limit when you have lost a piece of your heart.

It may seem after reading all of this, that the holidays will be horrendous. Yes, you may have some difficult times, but you certainly can experience some joy as well.

Having a good time and laughing does not mean you have forgotten your loved one or that you loved him/her any less.

Just remember, Anticipation of any holiday, birthday, or anniversary is much worse than the actual day.

So, take a breath, relax and try to enjoy what you can and the rest will take care of itself. Blessing to all of you!!!!!!!!!!!!!!!!!!!!!

TRIGGERS—ANNIVERSARIES, BIRTHDAYS, HOLIDAYS

What are **Triggers?** Triggers or "grief spasms" as they are often called, occur when everything seems to be going along okay and the bereaved are finally beginning to feel they "have a handle" on their grief. It is at that point when an anniversary of a marriage, death or even when the diagnosis occurred that the bereaved seem to take one step forward and three steps back.

Birthdays and holidays seem to have the same effect on the bereaved as anniversaries and other special days, because for the bereaved it really makes no difference, it is still difficult. However, anniversaries, birthdays and holidays are not the only triggers that cause the bereaved to "shutter in their tracks."

Some examples are: A phone call from a business or telemarketer who wants to speak to Mr./Mrs. and the bereaved have to explain that their loved one has died. If it is a husband who has died and the widow explains that her husband died, then her security maybe at risk, because they now know that she is alone and could be very vulnerable.

When a magazine continues to arrive with the deceased's name on the cover and the bereaved spouse has already canceled the subscription. When the bereaved are walking down the street, in a store or at the mall and see someone from a distance, wearing the same outfit that their loved one wore and they think it could be them -- still alive.

When the bereaved are at church, driving or walking down the street and see a couple holding hands and realize that this is no longer possible for them with their loved one. Perhaps they are at the mall and smell someone's cologne and it was the exact cologne their loved one wore. Perhaps they just turned on the radio in their car and it is playing the song that their loved one enjoyed singing or dancing to.

You go to the store and run into someone you haven't seen in a while and they ask how your wife/husband is doing? You are grocery shopping and are passing the meat section and realize your loved one loved to eat steak and you begin to cry. Perhaps you are shopping and suddenly realize you are now shopping for one rather than two like you have in the past. It could be, you are out to dinner with friends at a place that you and your spouse used to go and the waiter or waitress asks where your loved one is because they haven't seen him around lately.

A rose bush has not bloomed since your loved one died and suddenly on their birthday it blooms beautiful roses again.

These triggers can go on and on for the bereaved and can cause a setback in their grief if they are not careful.

The anticipation of birthdays, anniversaries are often more troublesome than the actual event. What should the bereaved do when the birthday or an anniversary does happen? Do they ignore it or not say anything to anyone, do they go out to dinner with friends and raise a glass in memory of their deceased loved one, bring flowers to the cemetery, etc.? The answer is simple, it is up to each individual to decide what will bring them comfort at that time. Even doing nothing is something. Often just the anticipation of an event is worse the actual day.

However, with the holidays there are more constant reminders such as holiday decorations in all the stores, greeting cards on the shelves, holiday displays and discounts on toys and other gifts, holiday movies, Christmas trees being sold on every other street corner, discussion about gifts and parties. In other words, no matter where you go or what you do, you can't hide from the holidays before they arrive or try to make changes before the holidays actually arrive, or can you?

There are several ideas that can help the bereaved during the holidays as well as approaching birthdays and anniversaries. It is a matter of taking control back of the situation and being prepared:

1. The most important thing to do is have a **PLAN**. In fact, have plan A, B and even C, if necessary, it will help the day go smoother.
2. Talk with family and friends before the scheduled event to let them know how difficult this might be for you and that you might have to leave early.

3. You are not obligated to go to every party or any party- **You** decide.
4. If everyone always comes to your house for dinner---suggest their house or going out to dinner this year.
5. If you have always sent Christmas cards, decorated the house, or done a lot of baking, this might be the year for a change. Perhaps, you could either send no cards or not as many; don't decorate as much or not at all and instead of baking this year just go out and buy that pie or dessert.
6. **Take care of yourself and don't put expectations on yourself that will cause you additional stress.**
7. Do something to honor your loved one's memory such as giving money in their name to a charity they liked, having a mass said for them, lighting a candle in memory of them, having a scholarship set up in their name for a student in the same area as the deceased, donating books in their memory to a library if they loved to read.
8. Try very hard to keep only positive people around you especially during the holidays, and other special events in your life.
9. If you had been to a support group before, it might be a good idea to go again during the holidays for some extra support.

Dr. Camille Wortman (2009) warned of four holiday season dilemmas to be aware of:

1. **Being Happy and Cheerful:** There seems to be an expectation that everyone should be happy and cheerful during the holidays. Please allow yourself to feel what you want—happy, sad, cheerful, unhappy not what others expect of you.
2. **The Mine Field of Social Exchange:** The innocent comments of others may cause a great deal of pain to the bereaved. The bereaved can be thrown off by the comments of complete strangers by comments such as "Hope you and your family have a wonderful holiday." This sounds like a wonderful greeting but when someone has died this greeting is very difficult to hear.
3. **The Complexity of Decisions:** The bereaved must decide what to do and what not to do when it comes to dealing with decisions about family activities and rituals. For example, a simple gesture such as whether or not to hang a stocking of the young child that died or sending holiday cards to family and friends may cause problems for the bereaved.
4. **The Ambush:** These are events that are unexpected and unpredictable. They are often called grief attacks or zingers. An example by Noel and Blair (2000) is: a mother was taking out her Christmas ornaments and came across an ornament that her young son who died had made in kindergarten last year. It had his hand print on it. She was so overwhelmed she dropped to her knees and just sobbed.

Be aware of being ambushed and always have a plan, take control, and let family and friends know your wishes early.

Reference
Wortman, C. (2009). Getting through the holidays: Advice for the bereaved. *University of Phoenix: WGBH Educational Foundation and Vulcan Productions, Inc.*

DOES GRIEF STOP IN THE SUMMER TIME?

This might seem like a strange question, but the answer is NO! Grief takes as long as it takes, it has no deadline. The changing of seasons, the time of day, the day of the month or even the weather makes no difference to grief.

Grief doesn't care who you are, what you look like, how old you are, whether you are rich or poor or old or young, male or female—grief is grief and works in its own time.

I have heard people say, it is sunny today and it is the summertime, so I think I am through with my tears and grief and ready to move on. That would be wonderful if it were true for everyone. However, grief has no boundaries and could care less about the weather.

Summertime can be a wonderful time, but often the activities, and the trips, you and your loved ones were planning to go to, were in the summertime and now you are alone or planning a trip without them, thinking you will have a wonderful time and perhaps you will, but be prepared if grief joins you on your trip.

One of the problems people have who are grieving is that one never knows when grief will strike again.

There are many incidences that can happen when they least expect it and then, the bereaved seem to take one step forward and two steps back-just when they were finally beginning to feel they are able to deal with how they are feeling.

These feelings can come and go but unfortunately, they can last for many years especially when we least expect it.

What can you do when something unexpectedly happens or you see someone unexpectedly and they ask about your deceased loved one, or perhaps someone calls and asks to talk with them or perhaps, you are in the grocery store and you are at the meat counter and realize your loved one loved steak and you just break down in tears etc.?

One way to deal with these "sudden cloud bursts" in your life is to take a deep breath, think for a moment, wipe away the tears (if there are any) and move on. If you need to answer someone on the phone, or someone you encounter while you are out somewhere, do the best you can do and move on.

It does not mean that you are sick, crazy, need a therapist, or psychiatrist, it just means you had a "sudden cloud burst" in your life and you will and can get through it now and in the future.

Just remember, when you have lost a part of your heart there is no time limit to your grief. Take as long as you need to get through the loss of your loved one whether it is a person or a beloved animal and don't let others rush you through your grief and tell you should be doing better than you are.

It is okay not to be okay!!! Everyone grieves differently. If the way you are grieving is helping you and working for you, then it is the right way for you to grieve the death of your loved one.

However, if you are struggling and having a difficult time, perhaps you might consider getting some help from a grief group or an individual grief therapist. Many times, it just helps to Talk with someone who will Listen and not judge you.

REMEMBER, GRIEF TAKES AS LONG AS IT TAKES!!!!!!!!! And the season, weather, time of day does not matter to GRIEF.

Milton Keynes UK
Ingram Content Group UK Ltd.
UKHW030745071024
449371UK00006B/539